A STUDY GUIDE TO

MASTERING *the art of*

Personal

EVANGELISM

With notes for individuals and group leaders

HOW TO BECOME A BOLD AND POWERFUL WITNESS FOR CHRIST IN EASY STEPS

APOSTLE/PASTOR GLEN E. KERR

W|K

Word of Knowledge Publishing

A Study Guide to—Mastering the Art of Personal Evangelism
Glen Kerr

Published by Word of Knowledge Publishing

www.wordofknowledge.com

==================
DEDICATION
==================

This study guide is dedicated to the body of Christ, and in particularly those who are willing and ready to equip themselves, to reach the lost for Christ in fulfilment of the Great Commission.

TABLE OF CONTENTS

==================

FOREWORD

==================

Have you ever picked up a book and got extremely excited to read through? Then you found out that the book was not coherent; very informative and inspiring but only up to a point. This is where the book in your hand is different. From start to finish, you will learn basic, yet profoundly inspiring nuggets that can make you a skilled soul winner and an expert on evangelism. Apostle Glen's blend of practical insight and purposeful guidance brings soul-winning alive and makes the dream of personal evangelism attainable by every believer.

Two main obligations given by Jesus Christ, and which have been accepted in the Christian world as essential, are the Great Commandment and the Great Commission. Both are important but differ in many ways. One deal with character building and relational issues and the other focus our minds on Kingdom business and Kingdom building. The former is the individual assignment and the latter is our corporate cum personal responsibility. Together, they account for the simple reason why, after our conversions, we are retained on Earth, at most for a period. God keeps us around so He can transform us 'into the same image' of His Son and also to engage us as His able and worthy 'Ambassadors'.

Jesus was remarkably clear about His assignment, "For the Son of Man came to seek and to save what was lost" (Luke 19:10), yet the Church is flippant of our corporate responsibility to "go and make disciples of all nations" (Matthew 28:19).

So we can be effective in our assignments, God has given us leaders and trainers, teachers and counsellors, coaches and mentors who have walked the path we dread and are also willing to take us with them. Apostle Glen is one of them. His deep love for the lost and profound understanding of principles of soul-winning earns him an authority on the subject.

A Study Guide To: Mastering the art of Personal Evangelism comes with notes for individual and group study. It takes you through the intricacies of personal evangelism; as little as speaking to your own family members to the more complex issues of personal sacrifices. It helps you deal with the fear factor; how to initiate a contact; and how to deal with difficult questions without getting entangled in unrewarding chatter.

Used together with '**Mastering the art of Personal Evangelism**', this study guide will propel you to the level of an expert soul-winner within weeks.

Sam O. Adewunmi
Pastor and Author, Good Finish to Bad Start

INTRODUCTION

========================

Rapidly Declining
21st Century Church

========================

This study guide will provide you the basic, easy to follow yet extremely essential principles that will revolutionize your thinking and radically change your approach when it comes to personal evangelism.

It will help you discover how simple it is to approach and share the gospel of Christ with just about anyone you meet. Beginning in your home, to neighbors, friends, work colleagues, fellow students etc. and to the wider community and the world at large.

The proven successful principles you will learn in the following pages, will build up your confidence, and provide you with full assurance that will work wonders, as you apply your faith with the help of the Holy Spirit to fulfil your divine destiny and purpose as a witness for Christ.

The essence of this study guide is to open up your mind to the solutions for overcoming the ancient predicament of fear and anxiety when it comes to what I would like to classify as the most shunned ministry in the Body of Christ. Follow the principles set out in this study guide and you will develop the freedom to tell the world about Jesus with boldness and confidence.

Solution for the Rapidly Declining 21st Century Church

Did you know that the 21st Century Church is in a rapid state of decline? If you do, have you ever wondered why?

Recent statistics proved that, in the USA alone, 85 percent of churches are declining. It has been said that, "When you measure church growth against population growth, only about 4% of churches in America are actually growing (that means 96% of churches are actually declining)... And, according to the Barna Group (An evangelical Christian polling firm based in Ventura, California), of the more than 350,000 Protestant churches in America, over 60,000 do not have a single convert each year."

The principal reason given for the rapid decline in church growth is summed up appropriately by Wes Moore, founder of Evidence America. He suggested that there are no strategies to recruit and train new believers within most congregations. "We don't organize our people to effectively reach the lost. Over 90% of our people have absolutely no intention of sharing their faith, and our leaders are often too apathetic to make any worthwhile changes".

> There are no strategies to recruit and train new believers within most congregations. "We don't organize our people to effectively reach the lost.

This is a tragedy especially since Jesus gave specific instructions to the Church in Matthew 28:19 to "Go, therefore, and make disciples of all nations..." Evidently, the 21st Century Church has fallen way short of the Great Commission, but it doesn't have to be this way.

You are holding in your hand a vital tool for equipping the saints for the spread of the gospel. In 2011, inspired by God, I wrote a book **"Mastering the Art of Personal Evangelism."**

This book sets out a number of basic, yet profound:

- **Principles**—on how to approach and talk to anyone without fear or intimidation;
- **Strategies**—to approach and talk to people about their eternal destiny even if you have no formal educational or even theological background;
- **Techniques**—for answering difficult questions and;
- **Proven outreach methods**—on how to win over anyone from atheist to Muslim; scientist to even your friends.

Having no strategy is not the only reason for the decline in church growth. Recent surveys also proved that personal evangelism is not a priority for most 21st century believers. It's almost like a curse word, guaranteed to drive fear into the hearts of thousands of Christians across the globe whenever it is mentioned. We know we've got good news to share but are doing very little to get the word out, and this was the sentiment Jesus echoed in Matthew 9:37 "The harvest truly is plentiful, but the laborers are few, therefore, pray the Lord of the harvest to send out laborers into His harvest." This is a good place to begin, we must pray to the Lord for more laborers.

> "The harvest truly is plentiful, but the laborers are few, therefore pray the Lord of the harvest to send out laborers into the harvest."

Reasons for the Lack of Enthusiasm

So what then do you think are the main reasons for the lack of enthusiasm when it comes to personal evangelism? First, it has to do with the lack of awareness and training. Many more people would become involved in witnessing for Christ if they only knew how and—this is the objective of this study guide.

It will help you to understand how to deal with such things as:

- Fear;
- How to initiate contact, and;
- How to deal with difficult questions—together with other vitally important factors responsible for driving fear into the hearts of believers when it comes to sharing their faith.

Over the last few decades, the Lord has raised up some great men such as Billy Graham, Morris Cerullo, Reinhard Bonnke and Benny Hinn to name but a few. These men have dedicated their lives to missions that have impacted the world and brought millions into the kingdom of God through awe-inspiring ways. I believe, however, that in this end time harvest of souls, God wants to raise you up, yes, you; God wants you to become the next life-transforming agent that will with ease, change the eternal destiny of the lost, the dying and those heading for destruction.

If you are ready, come with me and let me show you how you can become a bold and powerful witness for Christ in easy steps.

MAKING THE MOST
OF THIS STUDY GUIDE

Before I take you through these easy to follow techniques and principles, set out below are some valuable directives on how to make the most of this study guide not to be ignored. Read through each point very carefully and follow the instructions.

Inasmuch as you will find this study guide of great benefit when it comes to sharing your faith—if you are going to maximize your full potential as a witness for Christ, you need to get a copy of the main book, **Mastering the Art of Personal Evangelism** hereafter referred to as the manual. This will give you maximum and appreciable effectiveness and understanding of the principles taught in this study guide.

Suggestions for Individual Study

1. As you begin your study, pray that God will speak to you through His word and open your heart to receive the teachings of this study guide.

2. Read the instruction and introduction to each section/chapter and answer each question that follows. Answers to each question are at the back of the study guide. This is an in-depth study on personal evangelism, designed to help discover for yourself;

   a. The need to make personal evangelism a priority, and;

   b. To help you understand how easy it is to do.

3. The first half of this study guide provides you with an in-depth study into the reasons personal evangelism is the absolute priority for every believer. The objective of the author is to provide a strategy to help you fully understand and appreciate the need for this kind of equipping and training of believers to fulfil the Great Commission so that they can help others find their eternal destiny and purpose. Probably more important, to reap the high reward that comes from knowing Christ. Please do not be tempted to skip over these important instructions, it is important to take time and read it through thoroughly.

4. If you are serious about personal evangelism, as I have said in the introduction, it would be advisable to refer to the manual **"Mastering the Art of Personal Evangelism"** to which this study guide relates, in order to obtain full understanding and appreciation of each topic. Questions are built on the principles taught in the manual backed up by relevant scriptures.

5. Each chapter includes a number of questions which are intended to help you understand the dynamics behind the art of sharing your faith. Write your answers to the questions in the space provided or in a personal journal. Writing gives you clarity and deeper understanding of the Bible text together with the concept of the relevant section.

6. Always use prayer to guide and in thanking God for what you have learned and the wisdom on how to apply it.

Suggestion for Members of a Study Group

1. Always come to the study prepared. Follow the suggestions for individual study mentioned above. You will find that careful preparation will greatly enrich time spent in group discussion.

2. Be willing to participate in the study. The leader will not be lecturing; instead, he or she will be encouraging the members of the group to discuss what they have learned. The leader will be asking the questions that are found in this manual.

3. Stick to the topic being discussed. Your responses should be based on the relevant section together with the scripture references—which are the focus of the conversation.

4. Be sensitive to the other members of the group. Listen attentively when they explain what they have learned. You may be surprised by their insights. Each question may assume a variety of responses. Many questions may not have "right" answers, particularly questions that aim at meaning or application. Instead, the questions should push you to explore more thoroughly.

5. Be careful not to dominate the conversation. We are sometimes so eager to express our views that we leave little opportunity for others to respond. By all means, engage, however, also allow others to participate.

6. Expect God to teach you through the relevant scriptures used to back up specific views being expressed through

the other members of the group. Pray that you will have a profitable and enjoyable time as you discuss together.

7. Remember that nothing said in the group regarding the concept of this study is considered confidential so feel free to discuss outside the group, unless stated otherwise.

= CHAPTER ONE =

A Most Unpopular
Christian Ministry

When it comes to personal evangelism; most believers do not wish to get involved. Statistics shows that 95% of all Christians have never won a single soul for Christ, and 80 percent do not witness on a regular basis. Less than 2% are involved in evangelism, and 71% do not contribute toward any evangelistic outreach whatsoever. Most are of the opinion that personal evangelism should be left to those with special gifts, special callings, and special titles. But that is not the case: witnessing is the duty of every believer in Christ.

I am well aware of the challenges associated with witnessing, especially to those in your immediate circle. However, it is a tragedy that many have never attempted to share the need for salvation with their families, neighbors, friends, fellow students or colleagues.

Even some of those who have been in the church for years and hold positions of influence are often very uncomfortable sharing their faith. The truth is, if you really love the Lord and believe that hell is a real place where unbelievers spend eternity without remedy, you should be passionate about sharing the Gospel to save them from such a tragic end.

One of the primary reasons personal evangelism is the most unpopular ministry in the local church is that, most believers are not aware it is their duty to do so, or they do not know what to do and indeed, how to do it. **Hosea 4:6** says, "My people are destroyed for lack of knowledge."

There is also a general belief among believers that you do not need to tell anyone about Christ as they will see it by the life you live, but **Romans 10:14-17** disagrees:

> "How then shall they call on Him in whom they have not believed? And how shall they believe in Him of whom they have not heard? And how shall they hear without a preacher? And how shall they preach unless they are sent? As it is written: "How beautiful are the feet of those who preach the gospel of peace, who bring glad tidings of good things!" But they have not all obeyed the gospel. For Isaiah says, "Lord, who has believed our report?" So then faith comes by hearing, and hearing by the word of God."

Notice that faith does not come by mere observation but by hearing.

Other reasons personal evangelism is considered unpopular are the following discussion points. Read each point and discuss why, in your opinion, you believe personal evangelism is so unpopular among believers. (Please refer to the manual **"Mastering the art of Personal Evangelism"** for further details and analysis), then answer the questions that follow.

- Lack of awareness (pp24-25)
- Feelings of unworthiness and/or guilt (pp25-26)
- Ashamed to be identified with Christ (p24)
- Unaware of the urgency to reach the world for Christ (pp26-29)
- Lack of preparation (p29)
- Lack of conviction (pp30-31)
- Political correctness (p31)
- Don't know how to witness (p32)

The entire list above is dealt with in details, in the manual, but if you do not have one, you can brainstorm with other members of your group—if you are having a group discussion.

Questions:

1. Witnessing is to be left to people with unique gifts, talents and titles. True/False

2. Why Has God put you in your place of employment/ school right now?

3. What percentage of believers do not regularly witness for Christ?
95%
80%
2%

4. What percentage of believers has never won a single soul for Christ?
95%
80%
2%

5. Name 5 reasons given in this chapter for the lack of enthusiasm.

6. You should not, have to tell anyone about God, because they should see it in your life. True/False (discuss)

_____

7. What scripture cited in this chapter states that we must speak to others about their need for salvation?

_____

8. What is the main reason for the feeling of unworthiness that prevents most Christians from witnessing?

_____

9. How does the enemy use the past to hinder believers from witnessing?

_____

10. How can your past be used as an effective witnessing tool?

_____

11. What was the urgent call that Jesus made in John 4:35?

_____

12. What percentage of American Churches is growing in real terms?

_____

13. Why is God crowded out of a central position in human thoughts and values?

14. The world is desperate for the gospel. True/False (discuss)

Personal Notes

= CHAPTER TWO =

Knowing you are Called to be a Witness

Suppose I was to tell you that most believers do not know they have been called to be witnesses! This is a fact and is one of the reasons for the lack of personal evangelism in the local church.

Most church organizations identify and acknowledge the evangelist as one of the five-fold ministry gifts mentioned in **Ephesian 4:11**, but that is where it ends. The Church is doing very little to make their members aware that it is our responsibility as believers to spread the good news to those who are lost. We are all called to be witnesses onto Him and you are not exempt, therefore, I would like to help you understand that you are very much a part of this important mandate. If you are to comprehend this, you must understand the divine call of God upon your life with absolute clarity.

Understanding the Call

When I ask people if they are aware of the call of God on their lives, they usually give a confused look and a vague answer. They usually say, "I'm not sure" or "I don't know." The truth is that many believers are unsure of the reason they are here. Well, let me make something clear, you are not here merely to take up space until you die. You must be about your Father's business—of reflecting the love of Christ and sharing the good news of salvation.

In that regard, you must understand the two types of calls upon your life: the specific call and the general call.

The Specific Call

A specific call is one that is unique to you as an individual and takes into account your unique gifts and talents. This is often identified by a natural propensity to perform an assigned task with ease and great joy as if it is part of your DNA. Refer to the manual for further information on this area (pp38-39)

The General Call

The general call is a responsibility of every believer such as, the call to holiness and the call to win the lost. These calls do not require acknowledgement or affirmation; Jesus said it, so it is. Bottom line is, it is your duty as a disciple of Christ. Therefore, you are to do what God has called you to do with all your heart, all your soul, all your mind.

Once again, for a more in-depth study, please refer to the manual (pp39-42) and read the following bible passages and discuss.

- Matthew 5:15-16
- Acts 1:8
- 1 Peter 3:15
- Matthew 28:19
- Acts 22:15
- Matthew 5:13

Questions

1. Name the two types of calls mentioned in this chapter.

2. Name two reasons why witnessing is the most feared ministry in the Body of Christ.

3. What is a specific call?

4. What is a general call?

5. What are the main reasons witnessing is unpopular among believers?

6. What can be done to help you understand a specific call?

7. What is the fundamental lesson taught by Habakkuk?

8. What immediately happened when Habakkuk chose to listen?

9. What did God say to Habakkuk?

10. What is a good example of a general call?

11. What was Paul's advice to Timothy concerning the use of words?

12. How did Paul speak to the Corinthians?

13. "And I brethren, when I came to you I came not with the excellence of speech, declaring to you the testimony of God." What does this verse mean? (p41)

14. What will happen if we reject the knowledge of God?

Personal Notes

_____

_____

_____

_____

_____

= CHAPTER THREE =

Knowing Your Identity
as a Witness for Christ

Ambassadors for Christ

There is a serious identity crisis in the Body of Christ. Most believers do not know who they really are and to whom they belong. And while the vast majorities are aware of the need to know their identity, they inadvertently go about finding it the wrong way. Here is what I mean; many of us think about our identity from a positional perspective. Many think that having a position in a local church may establish their identity in the kingdom of God. For this reason, many aspire to be leaders of one type or another, and if they do not get their desired position, some even throw tantrums, disrupt programs and leave the church with an attitude. The reason for this kind of reaction is that such actions threaten their self-image. If such things are what define us, we will feel worthless if the position is denied.

The fact is, your title is not your true identity; your true identity is who you really are behind the facade. According to scripture, you are a witness, an ambassador for Christ—and quite frankly, titles do not get bigger than this. The thing is, for the title of an ambassador, you do not require the authenticity of any earthly authority. You have already been commissioned by God and no one can overturn it or take it away. The only one who can render it meaningless is you—this is if you fail to operate in your calling as an ambassador.

For a greater understanding of the life and calling of an ambassador, please read chapter three (reference manual pp46-

54.) If you do not have a manual, you can conduct your own research.

Discussion points

- Who is an ambassador? (reference manual pp46-48)
- How does an ambassador represent his/her country? (reference manual p48)
- The role of an ambassador (pp49-50)
- The characteristics of an ambassador (p51)
  - Not arrogant by nature (p51)
- How ambassadors respond to opposition (p52)
  - Ambassadors do not take offence personally (discuss) (pp52-53)

In summary, an ambassador must not be quick to respond to conflict. Must learn to forgive and forget and, must represent the kingdom with diplomacy and distinction

Understanding who you are in the kingdom will build your confidence as you assume your position as an ambassador for Christ.

Questions

1. To what secular profession is a witness likened in this chapter?

_____

2. Who is an ambassador?

_____

3. You have to be appointed by your local pastor before you can become an ambassador for Christ. True/ False

4. How does an ambassador represent his country?

5. What is the role of an ambassador?

6. What is the believer's role as an ambassador for Christ?

7. When does someone need the help of an ambassador?

8. How does the answer to question seven apply to an ambassador for Christ?

9. What did Paul say in 2 Corinthians 5:16 – 21 about how we are regarded as Christians?

10. Name 5 character qualities of an ambassador.

11. How do ambassadors respond to opposition?

_____

Personal Notes

_____

_____

_____

_____

_____

_____

_____

_____

_____

_____

_____

_____

_____

_____

_____

_____

_____

_____

_____

_____

= CHAPTER FOUR =

Understanding your
Motive for Witnessing

If you are going to be an outstanding witness capable of leading people to Christ on a regular basis, you must first determine your motive for witnessing. For instance, you will have to decide whether your motive is out of obligation to your church organization or out of loving obedience to Christ, or whether your motive is to force others or gently lead them to the truth.

Do not fail to understand the purpose of witnessing, which is to provide evidence based on personal knowledge/experience of the love of Christ—so others can understand God's incredible love and fall in love with the Savior who paid for their redemption. The greatest of zeal and intention will fall way short of the goal to win souls for the kingdom of God.

Here are the reasons for and against and discussion points on the motives for witnessing:

- The purpose for witnessing is not with intent to indoctrinate or for religious reasons—discuss. (pp62-63)

- The purpose for witnessing is not to impress others— Read notes on (pp63-65) together with 1 Corinthians 2:1-5: and discuss bearing in mind how Paul acted.

- We witness because of the value of the soul. Ecclesiastes 7:2 "Death is the destiny of every man, and the righteous should take it to heart" (pp67-69).

This is a universal question for which man has sought the answer since the beginning of time—the question of what happens to those who have gone on before and whether we will see them again. It is also every man's desire to know that his life has meaning and purpose, and he is desperate to know whether or not death is the end or merely the beginning of something else.

Study this section and pay particular attention to the following:

- o The most common Christian belief regarding life after death
- o The opinion of other civilizations
- o The opinion of pagan Greek philosophers such as Socrates, Plato, and Aristotle

Here are some of the reasons we witness:

- We witness because the message of salvation is good news (pp69-70)
- We witness to testify of what we know about Jesus (pp70-71)
- We witness because we are commissioned by Christ to do so. (p74

It is vital to be aware of your objective when it comes to witnessing. Your primary purpose is to share the love of Jesus, as opposed to the promotion of your particular church organization's agenda.

It is not a platform from which to argue doctrinal issues or prove how much you know. The question of arguing is addressed specifically in **2 Corinthians 10:4-5:**

> "For though we walk in the flesh we do not war according to the flesh, for the weapons of our warfare are not carnal but mighty in God for the pulling down of strongholds, casting down arguments and every high thing that exalts itself against the knowledge of God."

Notice here that the sole motive for witnessing is to tell the world about Christ and His death on the cross for the salvation of mankind, not for any other reasons.

Questions

1. What are the objectives of a witness?

_____

2. What important criteria should be used when dealing with those who are immature?

_____

3. Name at least 3 ways Paul acted when he preached to the Corinthians.

_____

4. Name 3 reasons why we witness.

_____

5. One of the motives for witnessing is to indoctrinate. True/False

6. The teaching of your church organization is more important than helping someone come to Christ. True/False

7. To be religious is the same as being godly. True/False

8. Devil worship is a religion. True/False

9. Every true ambassador has full confidence in his own ability. True/False

10. The gospel of Christ must be preached with simplicity and clarity. True/False

11. Why did Paul purpose in his heart to preach nothing but Christ and Him crucified?

12. The concept of life after death is strictly a Christian philosophy. True/False

---

Personal Notes

_____

_____

_____

_____

_____

_____

_____

_____

_____

_____

_____

_____

_____

_____

_____

_____

_____

= CHAPTER FIVE =

═══════════════

Understanding
How to Witness

═══════════════

Now, this is where we get down to the nuts and bolts of witnessing. In the previous chapters, we've discussed the reasons why we should witness; the importance of knowing we are called to be witnesses; the need to know and understand our identity as witnesses for Christ; and the importance of understanding our motive for witnessing. In this section, we will look at how to master the art of personal evangelism from a practical perspective. I will help you discover why you can and should witness like experts, the spirit in which witnessing should be conducted, and what support you have at your disposal to get the job done fearlessly and successfully. Following which we will look at the all-important areas of (1) how to deal with fear (2) how to initiate contact, and (3) how to deal with difficult questions.

Let me assure you that ordinary people like you and I can become expert witnesses. The thing is, there are specific requirements that must be met to be considered as experts. For example, to be qualified as an expert you must be knowledgeable and well-versed on your subject. Wikipedia, the online encyclopaedia describes an expert as;

> "Someone widely recognised as, a reliable source of technical skill, whose faculty for judging or deciding rightly, justly, or wisely is accorded authority and status by their peers or the public in a specific, well-distinguished domain"

Generally an expert is someone with extensive knowledge or ability based on research, experience or occupation in a particular area of study. A person is also considered an expert by virtue of credentials, training and education, profession. **But,** an expert can also be a person of experience believed to have knowledge of a subject beyond that of the average person, sufficiently that others may rely upon that person's opinion. Do you understand why an expert is, therefore, not necessarily the highly educated? A farmer with over forty years' experience of sowing seeds and tending flocks would be widely recognised as having complete expertise in the use of times and seasons

> An expert is also a person of experience believed to have knowledge of a subject beyond that of the average person, sufficiently that others may rely upon that person's opinion.

for sowing and reaping, and the care of animals. You can therefore become an expert in the area of witnessing for the reasons mentioned.

Many believers are waiting for a particular season of anointing to arrive to encourage them to preach the gospel with power. But the time for waiting is past. The fields are white unto harvest, and the Holy Spirit is already here, waiting for us to step out in faith and speak, because, at that point, He will fill our mouths with anointed words as we simply move in obedience.

Here is a summary of the main points you should have acquired from understanding how to witness for Christ. Regardless of your background or expertise you can witness with meekness and love in the power of the Holy Spirit.

a. Although we should do everything with excellence and be as well-prepared as possible that doesn't mean, we have to have a degree on the subject to become an expert.

b. We are never alone when witnessing, because Jesus promised the Holy Spirit would be our constant companion equipping us for every good work.

c. Because God's answers are always "Yea and amen" to the requests of those who seek Him with all their hearts, souls and minds, He will empower us when we fall in love with Him, hungry for the power and boldness to win souls, for this is His greatest desire.

d. Irrespective of our individual abilities and backgrounds, we are guaranteed to be able to witness like experts provided we do so with a spirit of meekness and love.

e. An expert is a person with extensive knowledge and experience based on research, but it is also based on prolonged, intense experience through practice. In other words, we don't need academic qualification to be classified as experts.

f. We are never alone when witnessing because we will always have the presence of the Holy Spirit with us.

g. Hunger for the things of God will empower us and give us boldness to witness.

Read chapter 5 of the manual and discuss the following.

Discussion Points

a. We are to witness like experts, discuss (pp79-80)

b. Witnessing should only be done with a servant's heart. Read Philippians 2:3-11 and discuss (pp80-82)

c. You have divine help (Joshua 1:1-9, Acts 1:4-8). (pp82-86)

Questions:

1. How does a person become classified as an expert?

2. Is it necessary for an expert to have professional or academic qualifications? True/False

3. In what spirit should we witness?

4. In what spirit should we not witness?

5. Why is it necessary to witness in love and compassion?

6. According to Matthew 28:19-20 Jesus left us a command and a promise. What was the command?

7. What was that promise?

8. Why did Jesus tell the disciples to go and wait for the Holy Spirit to come?

Personal Notes

= CHAPTER SIX =

How to Prepare Yourself To Witness

Make no mistake about it; it will take preparation and planning to make a lasting impact on the world when it comes to the salvation of souls. In other words you will have to be proactive about it, for example;

Read and discuss the following points

- You have to want to do it (Reference Manual pp90-91)
- You must be a student of God's word (Deuteronomy 30:11-14, Psalm 37:30-31, Psalm 119:11) (pp91-93)
- You must be willing to make yourself available for the Master's use (pp93-94)
- Your loudest evangelical voice must be your example (p94)
- You should never be ashamed of the gospel (p95)
- You must stay in control and manage your conversation (pp95-96)
- Be prepared to take it outside your comfort zone (p96)
- Must be determined and persistent (p97)

  As previously mentioned, if you are going to become an expert in witnessing, just like anything else you will have to believe in what you are aspiring to be, in other words, you must be driven by determination and persistence if you are going to succeed.

It is said that success is 1% inspiration and 99% perspiration. Strictly speaking, although you may be gifted and talented, you will fail if you give up or give it less than your best effort.

- Finally, you will need spiritual wisdom for the task (1 Corinthians 2:8, Proverbs 2...). pp97-98

Questions

1. Name five of the nine methods given in this chapter, to prepare you to witness.

_____

2. What kind of debates should you avoid at all cost?

_____

3. Why are we called to walk worthy of Christ?

_____

4. What is the most common response from believers about witnessing?

_____

5. What is the best approach to take when starting out as a witness?

_____

6. What is described as your loudest evangelical voice?

_____

7. What percentage of inspiration and perspiration are required for success?

_____

8. Complete this sentence: Commitment will allow the Holy Spirit to lead you to...

_____

9. What kind of wisdom will you need if you are going to master personal evangelism?

_____

_____

Personal Notes

_____

_____

_____

_____

_____

_____

_____

_____

_____

= CHAPTER SEVEN =

Dealing with the Fear Factor

Fear – Your Biggest Enemy

I am sure that you have found yourself in a situation where you would like to witness to someone about Christ only to realize that you are consumed with fear.

Maybe you're fearful of where and how to begin and your mind races as you wonder what they will think, and whether they will reject you. If you have ever found yourself in that situation, do not despair—we have all been there. In fact, human beings are afraid of many things. For example, some fear heights, some fear the dark, and it is said that some even fear success—but one of mankind's greatest fears is the fear of rejection.

In this section, I will teach you how to witness with confidence, but first, I must warn you, like any other skill, conquering fear is a process and will not necessarily happen overnight. **So what is fear?**

One of the best definitions of fear I've ever heard is this acronym:

F	False
E	Evidence
A	Appearing
R	Real

Fear is a powerful thing—a tool the enemy uses that can actually capture the mind and cause false reality to appear real. And the truth is, most of us have our own share of fears, especially where witnessing is concerned. The only difference is that over time and with encouragement some of us have overcome it.

Fear of Rejection

The fear of rejection is the greatest hindrance of all when it comes to sharing your faith. When we speak of fear of rejection, we are talking of the irrational fear that others will not accept us for who we are, what we believe and how we behave.

Peer Pressure

One of the reasons for fear of rejection is peer pressure. Peer pressure is influence exerted on a person or group of persons by a person or group of persons in order to get you to do something you would not otherwise do under normal circumstances.

How then Does Fear Affect You?

i. Fear will cause you to doubt—and doubt will prevent you from being efficient and successful in all areas of your life.

ii. Fear affects behaviour—For instance, it produces little or no assertiveness. It will prevent you from speaking up and letting others know how you feel about issues, especially if you are of a different opinion.

What happens when you act out of fear of rejection?

- Those who care for you will feel you are pushing them away;

- And then there are those who will be more than willing to take advantage of you.

Why People Operate Out of Fear of Rejection?

I would invite you to brainstorm this point then consult the manual for other reasons and further suggestions.

Steps to Overcoming the Fear of Rejection

2 Timothy 1:7. "For God has not given us a spirit of fear, but of power, of love and a sound mind."

The term "sound mind" denotes good judgment, a disciplined thought pattern, and the ability to understand and make wise decisions based on self-control and self-discipline.

Here are some steps to take to overcome the fear of rejection:

- Under no circumstances should you ever take things personally.
- Try to define yourself independently of other people's opinions. For example, if you are rejected, take it as a challenge and learn to accept the situation.
- Try to become comfortable at being uncomfortable.
- The first step to conquering fear of witnessing is to speak out. **See 2 Timothy 1:8**
- You must be sold on your mission
- You must believe in yourself
- A practical way to deal with fear—is to become what I call an <u>opportunistic witness</u>. By this, I mean, always be

on the lookout for people who are likely to be more receptive to the gospel—see p114 of the reference manual for further details.

Questions

1. What is the main reason most people do not witness?

2. Name two types of fear that prevent people from witnessing.

3. Explain the acronym – F.E.A.R.

4. What motto might help you combat fear?

5. Name at least three ways that fear is likely to affect you.

6. What two types of reactions are you likely to encounter if you act out of fear of rejection?

7. According to **2 Timothy 1:7**, what kind of spirit has God not given us?

8. Name 3 steps to overcoming the fear of rejection.

Personal Notes

_____

_____

_____

_____

_____

_____

_____

_____

_____

_____

_____

_____

_____

_____

_____

_____

_____

= CHAPTER EIGHT =

How to Initiate Contact

So how then do you approach someone with the gospel with confidence and without fear? This is one of the greatest hurdles you must cross, if you are going to master the art of personal evangelism.

Let me remind you that you are an opportunist witness—that means you are always on the alert for that opportunity to share the glorious gospel of Christ as opportunities arise. If you can master the art of initiating contact, you will inadvertently conquer fear in the process.

The following are a few basic principles to help you make that all important initial contact with ease and without any fear whatsoever.

Principle Number 1 – Change your Language

In order for you to ease your way into becoming a bold and powerful witness for Christ and especially when it comes to initiating contact, I suggest you begin with those closest to you (at your homes, your schools or colleges or your places of employment etc.) then broaden your reach.

The best way to initiate a conversation about salvation with people you are already familiar, is to change the way you speak. In other words your conversation must be different. This was Paul's instruction to Timothy to be an example in word (in conversation) and conduct. How you speak and conduct yourself is pertinent to the effectiveness of your communication of the gospel especially to those close to home.

Change your language using terms such as "God bless you," "I will pray for you," etc. This will send a very strong message to your acquaintances regarding your spiritual disposition towards them. Notice I have not told you to go and bash them over the head about religion; neither are you forcing anyone to do anything against their will. Just simply change the way you speak, it will do wonders for you in this regard.

Principle Number 2 – Choose your targets

As you move out to talk to strangers, the first thing I would like you to understand is, until you have become more proficient in sharing the gospel, it is important that you realize that not everyone is ready to receive the gospel. With this in mind, it would be of no benefit to you to try to hold a conversation with an atheist or a scientific nerd at this stage. It is best to choose softer targets until your confidence develops. So, how do you choose a target? Rule number three explains.

Principle Number 3 – Find a need and fill it

Adopting an attitude of helping especially people who are in need is pertinent to your effectiveness as a witness for Christ. This concept is expertly illustrated in the story of The Good Samaritan as explained in the manual. (pp121-125) subsection 3 and 4.

Principle Number 4 – Establish the Basis for the Conversation

Take the initiative to be the first to speak so that you can set the tone of the conversation. (pp125-128)

Principle Number 5 – Establish a Common Ground

In the book of **John 4:8-15**—that famous story about the woman at the well, notice how Jesus established that common ground, He used the common denominator important to both of them at that point in time—water. (pp125-130).

One of the reasons it is important to establish common ground is Proverbs 23:9 says: "Do not speak in the hearing of a fool, for he will despise the wisdom of your words."

Principle Number 6 - Must Arouse Interest.

The importance of establishing a common ground is to make your conversations relevant to the person, the situation and the circumstances, and to arouse interest. The need to arouse interest is critical, and this is what we observe when we read the story in John 4. Again, Jesus speaking to the "woman at the well," aroused her interest by using water as a common denominator. (pp130-131)

Questions

1. Name three basic rules for how to initiate contacts.

_____

2. What famous Bible story was used to illustrate the question regarding who is your neighbor?

_____

3. When Jesus asked the lawyer who of the three persons was neighbor to the man who fell among thieves, what was the lawyer's answer?

_____

4. In your own words describe the lesson you can learn from the lawyer's reply.

_____

5. What was Jesus' instruction to the lawyer?

_____

6. What did Jesus send His disciples to do in Luke Chapter 9?

_____

7. What 2 important things did Jesus give to the disciples?

_____

8. When sharing the gospel, you will be well-received by everyone. True/False

_____

9. When sharing the gospel, you should show people you are only interested in their spiritual wellbeing. True/False

_____

10. Name two things you need to show when initiating contact.

_____

11. What familiar interest did Jesus use when establishing a common ground with the woman at the well?

_____

12. How did He do this?

_____

Personal Notes

_____

_____

_____

_____

_____

_____

_____

_____

_____

_____

_____

_____

_____

_____

_____

_____

_____

_____

= CHAPTER NINE =

How to Deal with Difficult Questions

The chances are that, at some time, or another, nearly everyone has talked with someone with a serious appetite for philosophy. The word "philosophy" actually means, love for knowledge. People with that bent tend to want to impress others at every opportunity. Their views are often twisted, especially in regard to religion. This is true even among Christians.

An excellent illustration can be found in Colossians 3, where Paul wrote concerning false teaching that was creeping into the Church. They had started to teach Greek philosophy and Jewish legalism, which were in essence undermining the authenticity of Christ and threatening to bring confusion and false teaching into the Church. This occurred because of the Greeks' love for knowledge and hence, resulted in a distorted view of what a believer should be. These kind of people tend to want to prove themselves by posing difficult questions.

As an inexperienced witness, you've probably wondered how to handle such difficult questions. Perhaps the thought makes you feel anxious. If so, let me reassure you that there is no need to be afraid. I will show you some basic strategies for how to deal with any tough questions you are likely to encounter.

The one thing I must emphasize here is that you have nothing to prove when witnessing. Reason being; it's not about you or even about man's wisdom. The wisdom that you require to carry out the task comes from God.

Strategy for answering difficult questions

When people ask difficult questions they are either searching for genuine answers or trying to refute what you have to say. In either case, the following rules/strategies apply:

Strategy Number 1- Be Honest

When a person is seeking genuine answers, you will probably not find them too awkward to deal with. This is because you have already convinced them of their need of salvation or, if they are not yet fully persuaded they possess a genuine heart that is leaning toward the truth. On the other hand, most of the people who are likely to pose difficult questions with intent to test your knowledge are likely to fall into one of the following categories:

- People from different religious backgrounds
- Atheists
- Agnostics
- Scientists
- Those with no religious persuasion whatsoever.

Difficult questions can arise due to the diversity of peoples' backgrounds, and it may be hard to understand their motivation. But once again, honesty is always the best policy and will let them know you are a person of integrity. If you do not know the answer, do not be afraid to say so.

Strategy Number 2 - The Burden of Proof

Some of the most common and yet difficult questions are about the existence of God, evolution and creation, science, and other Bible subjects. If, for example, the question challenges the existence of God, the burden of proof belongs to the person asking the question. In other words, it is their responsibility to prove there is no God, not for you to prove there is one. (See witnessing to atheist in chapter 10 of the manual pp161-166 for further illustration.

Strategy Number 3 - Use Your Testimony

It may come as a surprise to you when I suggest that you use your testimony when answering difficult questions. The truth is, your testimony may not actually answer difficult questions. What it does, however, is that it shifts the pointing of the finger from the sinner and focus unto you and your personal experience with God. The one thing is, it must be a good and powerful testimony, and I am sure you have many of those.

A very practical example of a good testimony vs. a lazy person's testimony can be found in the book of John **Chapter 9:2-25.** Read this account and discuss with the other members of your group.

This is an awesome testimony; in essence, it does not matter what other people's opinions are: all I know is once I was blind but now I can see. What he was saying here is, the evidence of my testimony speaks for itself. Therefore, let the evidence of your testimony speak for you.

Strategy Number 4 - Avoid All Religious Conflicts

2 Corinthians 10:5 tells us, "There is a spirit in us that seeks to exalt itself against the knowledge of God." This character trait leads to arguments and debates and most importantly, the need to be right at all costs. This is very self-centered and therefore does not bring glory to God. Let's look at this in context, starting at verse 3:

> "For though we walk in the flesh, we do not war according to the flesh. For the weapons of our warfare are not carnal, but mighty in God for the

pulling down of strongholds. Casting down arguments and every high thing that exalts itself against the knowledge of God. Bringing every thought into captivity to the obedience of Christ and being ready to punish all disobedience when your obedience is fulfilled."

This passage teaches us that the war of the flesh includes strongholds, arguments, and every high thing that exalts itself against the knowledge of God, and should be avoided at all cost.

Questions

1. What kind of teaching was creeping into the Church in Colossae?

_____

2. What was the primary reason for this kind of teaching?

_____

3. Who is the supreme and unseen witness?

_____

4. What is the main function of the Holy Spirit?

_____

5. What is the answer to every important question in life?

_____

6. What was it Paul admonished Timothy not to do as a workman?

7. What lesson can we learn from the answer to question 6?

8. Complete the following Bible text: "All scripture is given by God for...)

9. What is the first rule for answering difficult questions?

10. Should someone try to lure you into a debate, for example, regarding whether or not there is a God, how should you respond?

11. How can your testimony be used when answering difficult questions?

Personal Notes

= CHAPTER TEN =

======================================

How to Witness To
Different Groups of Individuals

======================================

If you are to master the art of personal evangelism, it will be necessary for you to know how to deal with different groups of people. In order to have an amicable discussion; you may need a different approach for each group.

In this chapter, we will look at a select group, but the list is not exhaustive. We will consider the religious persons, your neighbors, those you know, those who are hurting, the atheists, the agnostics, and Muslims—this detailed background information will help you understand and relate to them more easily.

Witnessing to the Religious Person

If you have tried to witness to a religious person, I am sure you will agree that they are among the most difficult to reach with the gospel. Believe it or not, it is even more difficult when it comes to religious Christians, why? This is because they are generally people who hold firmly to their tradition and are not normally accommodative to anyone else's opinion. In essence, they think they are always right, and everyone else is wrong.

The most effective way to witness to a religious person is never to get side-tracked from the issue of salvation. (See chapter 11 "A Journey down the Roman Road to Salvation"). It is also imperative to emphasize the fact that everyone must be born again, **John 3:7.**

Witnessing to Those in Your Neighborhood

Those closest to us, including our families, friends, and neighbors are right up there with the religious people as the most difficult to witness to. Our neighbors are pretty much like family; we do not want to offend them unnecessarily because we have to live with them, and therefore we sometimes prefer to keep silent. The problem is, we cannot afford to have them next door and never seize the opportunity to share the gospel of Christ with them. In that regard, I would remind you of **Mathew 5:13-16**

> "You are the salt of the earth; but if the salt loses its flavor, how shall it be seasoned? It is then good for nothing but to be thrown out and trampled underfoot by men. You are the light of the world. A city that is set on a hill cannot be hidden. Nor do they light a lamp and put it under a basket, but on a lamp stand, and it gives light to all who are in the house. Let your light so shine before men that they may see your good works and glorify your Father in heaven."

In essence, we must abound in good works towards men, but especially to our neighbors. The Bible lets us know that this is a legitimate means of evangelism. According to **1 Peter 2:15** it is God's will that "with well doing you may put to silence the ignorance of foolish men." (pp155-156)

Witnessing to People You Know

As with witnessing to your neighbors, it is always much easier to witness to strangers than to those you know. But the following suggestions can be helpful:

Use Praise Reports

In the previous chapter when we discussed how to answer difficult questions, I told you your testimony could be used to great effects. That suggestion will also be applicable here. Praise reports are one of the most powerful means of communicating the message of salvation to the people you know, because a testimony speaks for itself.

Give Them a Point of Reference

The next suggestion is to give them a point of reference. Here is what I mean! Suppose you want to share the gospel with a work colleague or a fellow student you knew for a long time but have never seriously engaged in spiritual conversations, would you know where to begin? Maybe for you, these are people who do not understand and appreciate the seriousness of your commitment to God. Maybe the truth is that you were not that committed but now you are and feel you must reach them. I suggest that you arrive at work Monday morning with the goal of setting a new precedent. In a very excitable tone tell them, "I went to church yesterday," then explain how that experience changed your life. Explain that you have decided to make some significant changes to the way you live your life. From now on, make this a priority at every opportunity that arises. Once again, notice, Once again, notice, you are not telling anyone, anything about religion neither are you pointing an accusing finger at them. you are not telling anyone, anything about religion or pointing an accusing finger at them. You are merely sharing what God is doing in your life. This method works every time, guaranteed.

Use the First Person Approach

When witnessing to those who know our faults it's best to use the first person approach, saying something like: "Though I have attended church for ten years, I did not truly appreciate the power of God to change lives." Or if they are unbelievers, you might say, "I've attended church for some time but until now I never realized the Bible is the final authority regarding my eternal destiny." This is likely to induce one of two responses: First, it may arouse curiosity, or it will inevitably open up a floodgate of questions. Either way, it will serve as your opportunity to share the gospel.

Witnessing to those who are Hurting

There's a good chance that your greatest challenge will be to witness to those who are hurting. Why? Because they require special care and understanding. It will take all your resources to be effective and to exercise good judgment.

At all time, you must be very sensitive to the immediate need of the person who is hurting but at the same time you cannot afford to ignore the need for that person's salvation. Comfort them by sharing with them the amazing love of God, and assure them that God longs to comfort them in their time of need.

Witnessing to Atheists

From a personal perspective augmented by scriptures, I do not believe there is any such person as an atheist. Webster's Dictionary describes an atheist as someone "not believing in the existence of God or any other deity," but there is only one way to describe such a person who says there is no God— "a fool." Psalm 14:1 tells us: "The fool has said in his heart 'there is no God'; they are corrupt, they have done abominable works; there is none who does good." **Psalm 19 says;**

The heavens declare the glory of God; And the firmament shows His handiwork. 2 Day unto day utters speech, and night unto night reveal knowledge. 3 There is no speech nor language where their voice is not heard. 4 Their line has gone out through all the earth, and their words to the end of the world. In them He has set a tabernacle for the sun, 5 Which is like a bridegroom coming out of his chamber, and rejoices like a strong man to run its race. 6 Its rising is from one end of heaven, and its circuit to the other end; and there is nothing hidden from its heat. 7 The law of the Lord is perfect, converting the soul; The testimony of the Lord is sure, making wise the simple; 8 The statutes of the Lord are right, rejoicing the heart; The commandment of the Lord is pure, enlightening the eyes; 9 The fear of the Lord is clean, enduring forever; The judgments of the Lord are true and righteous altogether. 10 More to be desired are they than gold, Yea, than much fine gold; Sweeter also than honey and the honeycomb."

Listen to verses 11-13:

"Moreover by them your servant is warned, and in keeping them, there is great reward. Who can understand His errors? Cleanse me from secret faults. Keep back your servant from presumptuous sins; Let them not have dominion over me. Then I shall be blameless. And I shall be innocent of great transgression."

Here the Scripture is saying that the heavens declare God's glory and also proclaim His wisdom, His power, and His goodness. But listen to this, so that all ungodly men are left without excuse. Paul picks up the story in **Romans 1: 18-32** when he tells us, all mankind needs salvation, in that we cannot obtain the favor of

God or escape His wrath by our own works or believing whatever we please. The sinfulness of man is simply described as ungodliness "against the law of the first table" and "unrighteousness against those of the second," which make reference to the Old and the New Testament Scriptures. Just because someone says they do not believe in God, does not mean that God will in a fit roll up the heavens like a scroll and pack it away saying, "I can't be bothered" because they do not believe in Me. No matter what someone chooses to believe, will not cause heaven to cease, or cause the order of heaven to be disrupted.

Here Paul was emphasizing that it was their sin that was holding the truth in unrighteousness, doing what they knew to be wrong, while omitting what they knew to be right. He eliminated the ignorance as an excuse for sin. "Therefore you are without excuse" (**Romans 2:1**). They are without excuse because our Creator's invisible power and Godhead are so clearly shown in the works of His hand that even those who classify themselves as atheists, agnostics, idol worshippers, and the wicked are left with no excuse. Paul is saying that they foolishly followed idolatry, and rational creatures changed the worship of the glorious creator to that of brutes, reptiles, and senseless images. They wandered from God until all traces of true godliness were lost.

Amid the depravity of such irreligious concepts, the Word of the Lord was revealed. "Light was come into the world but men loved darkness rather than light (**John 3:19**)."

So why am I telling you all this? I am trying to get you to understand why the burden of proof is not on you but on that atheist—For a practical example please refer to p164 of the manual.

Witnessing to Agnostics

An agnostic is a person who believes that it is impossible to know whether there is a supreme being or God. In other words, the agnostic is sceptical about the existence of God. But while he is doubtful, he does not profess true atheism. Simply put, agnostics claim to have no knowledge of the existence of God. In fact, the term "agnostic" literally means "no knowledge." They do not have a commonly accepted set of views, so they chose to sit on the fence.

Once again the burden of proof is the approach to take when witnessing to the agnostics. For a practical illustration—Please refer to p168 of the manual.

Witnessing to Muslims

Perhaps you have heard the name "Muslim" but have no idea what it means or who they are. Here is some background information.

Islam is the world's second largest religion, with a following of approximately 1.3 billion people called Muslims.

Muslims can be found across the entire globe. And though they can be found in North and South America, the Caribbean, and Western Europe, they are mostly found in Africa, the Middle East, and Asia. According to Wikipedia, "Their most predominant homeland lies in the area commonly known as the 10/40 window" About 60% of Muslims are Asians. The regional breakdown of Muslims in the rest of the world is as follows: Arabs 22%, Sub-Sahara Africans 12%; Eastern Europe 5%, and the rest are scattered throughout the world.

Islam was founded in 610 A.D. by a man named Mohammed. During his time, people were worshipping multiple gods. The concept of worshipping many gods is known as polytheism. During one of Mohammed's trips as a trader, he claimed to have had a dream given to him by a being he perceived to be an angel who told him, "There is only one God, and his name is Allah. Worship him."

There are seven fundamental beliefs of the Islamic faith that every Muslim must accept as part of their religion (the Emanul Mufassil or faith listed in details). As part of their religious training, every Muslim must learn this formula.

1. "Belief in God, (who in Arabic, is named Allah)"
2. "Belief in the angels (both good and bad)"
3. "Belief in the revealed books of God"
4. "Belief in God's many prophets (including Adam, Abraham, Moses, David, and others Christians and Jews are familiar with)"
5. "Accepting that there will be a last day"
6. "Belief in the divine measurement of human affairs"
7. "Belief in life after death"

What Do Muslims Believe Saves Them?

Islam requires that its followers earn their way to heaven by performing the five pillars of the faith, as follows.

1. Say the confession of faith.

A Muslim must confess, "There is no God but Allah and Mohammed is the prophet of God."

2. Pray.

Muslims are supposed to pray five times a day: shortly before sunrise, mid-morning, noon, min-afternoon, and after sunset.

3. Give alms.

Muslims are to give about 5.5% of their wealth.

4. **Fast during Ramadan**.

For one lunar month, from sunrise to sunset, Muslims are not to allow anything to pass down their throats (theoretically speaking, good Muslims do not allow even the saliva to pass down; instead they spit it out). Then from sunset to sunrise, they are permitted to eat as little or as much as they want. This is their way of developing discipline and relating to the poor. (Travellers, young children, and pregnant or nursing mothers do not need to keep the fast.)

5. **Make pilgrimages to Mecca**.

Every Muslim, who is financially able, is supposed to travel to the birthplace of Islam once in their lifetime.

Do Muslims Have Any Guarantee of Salvation?

Muslims do not have any guarantee that they are saved. They believe that all their works will be accounted for and that on Judgment Day, if their bad work outweighs their good work, they will go to hell.

Is there Any Variation in Islam?

Believe it or not, Islam varies greatly around the world. Despite the fact that Muslims go to great length to describe themselves as members of the brotherhood of "one religion", the Islam practiced in say Africa—is far different from that which is practiced in Saudi Arabia, which is also different from that which is practiced in Iran, or Morocco. In fact there are no fewer than 72 different sects in Islam (as in denominations).

How Do Muslims View Christianity?

Most Muslims are of the opinion that Christians believe in three Gods: God the Father, God the Son and God the Mother (Mary). They believe that Christians and Jews have changed the Bible; therefore, although the Quran acknowledges the Gospel of Christ, the Torah of Moses and the Psalms of David, they believe the existing copies cannot be trusted. As a result, they believe that all these Holy Books are superseded by the Quran.

Why Is It So Hard to Lead Muslims to Christ?

Because of their culture and community! Muslims who want to turn to Christ feel a need to find a strong community of Christians where they can belong, before they will accept the truth. The problem is, in most Muslims areas, there are no acceptable Christian communities, which makes it very difficult for Muslims to follow Christ.

Are Muslims Coming to Know Christ?

The answer to the question as to whether Muslims are coming to know Christ is a resounding yes! It has been reported that since 1970, many more Muslims have come to know Jesus than at any other time in history. For further information, please refer to the manual p174.

In Review

- Whatever you do, whenever you witness, be courteous and loving at all times.
- Show a personal interest and remember to allow people to speak, let them articulate their views.

- It is helpful to understand their basic beliefs as set out in this chapter, but you may also want to investigate further. With regard to Muslims, you must be willing to examine and cross-reference the Quran with respect to their beliefs.

- It is a big plus to know also that the Quran acknowledges such fact as; Jesus is coming back again and the virgin birth, etc.

- Make sure you are aware of how the Quran refers to Christ—as the breath of God, the Spirit of God and the life of God.

- Stick to the doctrine of the Christian faith but also be sure to take time out to answer all genuine questions. I must emphasize again the need to be honest and say so if you don't know the answer.

- It is imperative that you place emphasis on the importance of Jesus in the process of salvation.

- Make it clear that because of Jesus, His death on the cross, and the resurrection from the dead, one may have the full assurance of salvation as set out in **1 John 5:13**.

- Clearly and coherently point out the plan of salvation, particularly that salvation is a gift and cannot be earned. **See Chapter 11.**

- Pray for the leading of the Holy Spirit during your time of witness. Depend on the Spirit to provide you with wisdom and grace.

- Most importantly, you must be willing to become a friend; in other words, let the beauty and the love of Jesus shine through you in a magnificent way. Remember, "It's not what you say but how you say it."

Questions:

1. Name four reasons why it is difficult to witness to a religious Christian.

_____

2. Jesus believed in sectarianism. True/False

_____

3. What verse of scripture given in Luke 9 proved that Jesus does not believe in sectarianism?

_____

4. What will be the most likely result if you get side tracked into debates?

_____

5. When witnessing to a religious person, what should be your aim?

_____

6. What is the best way to witness to people you know?

_____

7. What are the other two ways given to witness to people you know?

8. What is the most important tool for witnessing to the hurting?

9. When witnessing to someone who is hurting, it is okay to ignore the salvation of their soul. True/False

10. On whom is the burden of proof when witnessing to an atheist or agnostic?

11. Who founded the Islamic faith?

12. What is the name of the Islamic holy book?

13. Name three other holy books Muslims are supposed to read.

14. Name five things Muslims think about Jesus.

15. How do Muslims think they are saved?

16. Do Muslims have any guarantee of salvation?

Personal Notes

_____

_____

_____

_____

_____

_____

_____

_____

_____

_____

_____

_____

_____

_____

_____

_____

_____

= CHAPTER ELEVEN =

A Journey down the
Roman Road to Salvation

This piece of work will be incomplete without taking you down the Roman Road to salvation. The Book of Romans provides a simple yet profound explanation of the process of salvation. For example, Romans tells us:

a. The reason everyone needs salvation
b. How God made the provision for salvation
c. How we can receive salvation, and;
d. The benefits of obtaining salvation

It is important that you study this carefully because if you do not know anything else you will need to know how to explain why everyone needs salvation together with the other points mentioned above. You may also be required to help your new prospect accept Christ as Lord and Savior.

This will be very important when witnessing to unbelievers, but it may be even more appropriate when witnessing to religious Christians. Many people believe that they do not need salvation, because they are good people. They will tell you about the good deeds they have done and that they have not hurt anybody, etc. No doubt you have come across people like that. This is the reason we must place a strong emphasis on the truth that no one can earn their salvation by good works.

Let's travel with the apostle Paul as he addresses these issues in his letter to the Romans.

The Reason Everyone Need Salvation

The first question we must address is: why does everyone need salvation? Romans 3:23 has the answer: "For all have sinned, and fall short of the glory of God." This is indeed your first port of call. Should anyone ask you why they need salvation, your answer should be, because "we all have sinned." We all have done wrong and displeased God no matter how good we may consider ourselves to be. And just in case someone thinks they have no sin, Paul explains in Romans 3:10–18,

> "As it is written: There is none righteous, no, not one. There is none who understands; there is none who seeks after God. They have all turned aside; they have together become unprofitable. There is none who does good, no, not one. Their throat is an open tomb. With their tongues they have practiced deceit; the poison of asps is under their lips; whose mouth is full of cursing and bitterness. Their feet are swift to shed blood; destruction and misery are in their ways. And the way of peace they have not known. There is no fear of God before their eyes."

So clearly we all have sinned and fall short of God's glory. Thank God Paul did not just expose us to the fact that we all have sinned without letting us know of the consequences.

The second point I would like you to be aware of is, there is a penalty for the sins you have committed. **Romans 6:23** tells us, "For the wages of sin is death; but the gift of God is eternal life in Jesus Christ our Lord." There is a heavy price to be paid for sin and that is death and eternity in hell. Death and hell are the result of sin, and no one is exempt.

How God Made the Provision for Salvation

Paul then went on to say that, in spite of our sins, God made provision for our pardon. Look at the second part of **Romans 6:23:** "But the gift of God is eternal life through Jesus Christ our Lord." Hallelujah, thank God He has not left us to die in our sins. Paul did not stop there, because in **Romans 5:8** he tells us how God did it. "But God demonstrates His own love toward us, in that while we were still sinners, Christ died for us." Many people will tell you that all religions lead to God, but that is not the case. There is no remission for sins, no forgiveness, apart from the death of Christ on the cross. Why? Because Jesus, the perfect Lamb of God, had to die in our stead to pay the price to redeem us back to God.

How We Can Receive Salvation

Notice that the Apostle did not just give us information about the consequences of sin and the gift of God, but he also told us how to obtain salvation. This can be found in **Romans 10:9**: "That if you confess with your mouth the Lord Jesus, and believe in your heart that God has raised Him from the dead, you will be saved." This is a crucial piece of information because it tells the listener what he has to do—to first of all believe and then to confess Jesus as Lord. Can you see why witnessing is so important?—you are not only to believe, but you must also tell it, confess it, and bear witness of it. This is confirmed in **Romans 10:13**: "For whoever calls on the name of the Lord shall be saved." Thank God the forgiveness of sins is available to all who dare to trust Jesus as Lord and Savior.

The Benefits of Obtaining Salvation

Finally, the Apostle then completes the journey by speaking of the benefits of salvation. **Romans 5:1** tells us: "Therefore, having being justified by faith, we have peace with God through our Lord Jesus Christ." This is where man finally finds peace and redemption from his sinful nature. Besides, this gives full assurance of our place in the company of the people of God. The journey comes to a magnificent conclusion with **Romans 8:1**: "There is therefore now no condemnation to those who are in Christ Jesus. Who do not walk according to the flesh but according to the Spirit." Can you imagine that? Because of Jesus' death on the cross, you can never again be condemned for your sins. Then the Apostle capped this off with an incredible promise. which can be found in **Romans 8:38–39**: "For I am persuaded that neither death nor life, nor angels nor principalities nor powers, nor things present, nor things to come nor heights, nor depths, nor any other created things shall be able to separate us from the love of God which is in Christ Jesus our Lord."

What an awesome journey this has been. The journey started with a life full of sin, punishable by death and ended with full assurance of life more abundantly. Can you see why you must never be ashamed of the gospel of Christ? It is indeed the power of God unto salvation.

The Romans Road is an easy-to-use tool to understand what your salvation means, and should also be of great help when sharing the clear and easy-to-understand message of the gospel.

Prayer

Prayer should never be underestimated when leading a person to Christ. It is a declaration of that person's reliance on Christ alone for salvation. Keep in mind, however, that it is not the words of the prayer that save them, but the faith behind that prayer.

Following is a simple prayer you can use when leading your prospective convert to the Lord. Have them repeat it after you if they seem uncomfortable doing it alone.

"Lord, I know that I have sinned against you and am deserving of punishment. But Jesus Christ took the punishment that I deserve so that, through faith in Him, my sins can be forgiven. With Your help, I place my trust in You for salvation. Thank You for Your wonderful grace and forgiveness—and the gift of eternal life!"

In review we looked at:

- The process of salvation.
- Why everyone needs salvation?
- How God made the provision for salvation.
- How the unsaved can receive this salvation.
- The benefits of obtaining this salvation.

Questions:

1. What are the 4 fundamental principles taught in the Book of Romans?

2. Why is the Romans Road to salvation so important?

3. According to Jesus, there are good people in the world. True/False

4. According to Romans 3:23, why does everyone need salvation?

_____

5. What is the penalty for sin according to Romans 6:23?

_____

6. All religions lead to God. True/False

_____

7. Unless a person embraces the necessity for Christ's death on the cross, there is no remission of sins. True/False

_____

8. According to Romans 10:9, what two words describe how a person can receive salvation?

_____

9. According to Romans 10:13 who can be saved?

_____

10. How did the apostle Paul complete the journey of salvation? Romans 5:1

_____

11. Complete this verse. "There is therefore now no condemnation…

_____

= CHAPTER TWELVE =

Counting the Cost of Discipleship

U p to this point, I have shared a vast amount of information regarding personal evangelism. For example, I have told you how to conquer fear, how to make that all important initial contact, how to answer difficult questions, how to talk to people from all walks of life including atheists, agnostics, scientists and people from other religions and that's just to name but a few. What I have not told you is that it comes at a price. As with anything else, success does not come easily or cheaply. In other words, if you are going to succeed you must be prepared to pay the price.

First, let me remind you that in order to be a witness for Christ, you must be a disciple. There is no way you should even consider witnessing for the kingdom until you are a follower of Christ. And to be a disciple of Christ comes with a very high price. In fact, it should cost you your life. Notice the word 'should', because not many people are willing to give up their lives for the gospel. One way or another, you will have to pay with your life. If not physically, you will have to pay spiritually, but you have to die. Let me explain. Jesus said, "Except a grain of wheat falls to the earth and dies, it abides alone." (**John 12:24**) The only way you can be an ambassador for Christ is to be dead to the flesh and be alive in Christ. You cannot be dead to the flesh and be alive in Christ simply by being religious. You need to be a sold-out believer, not for selfish ambition or personal gain.

I grew up hearing about folks being so heavenly-minded they are no earthly good. For me, such a notion is preposterous. In fact, that has to be one of the enemy's biggest deceptions of our day. How can it be possible that one can be so heavenly-minded that he or she is no earthly good? This kind of mind-set is devilish, demonic, and straight from the pit of hell. Certainly, it is not a concept taught in the scriptures and most certainly it could not have come from a spirit-filled believer. If you are someone who believes that you can be too heavenly-minded, let me give you a few scriptures that will eliminate such rubbish from your mind.

Deuteronomy 6:5–6

> "You shall love the LORD your God with <u>all your heart, with all your soul, and with all your strength.</u>" Notice that it says "with all,"—not with part, but with all your heart, soul, and strength."

Later on in **Mark 12:30**, it reads:

> "<u>all your heart, all your soul, and all your mind.</u>" "And these words which I command you today shall be in your heart. You shall teach them diligently to your children, and shall talk of them when you sit in your house, when you walk by the way, when you lie down, and when you rise up."

Joshua 1:7-8

> "Only be strong and very courageous, that you may observe to do according to all the law which Moses My servant commanded you; do not turn from it to the right hand or to the left, that you may prosper wherever you go. This Book of the Law shall not

depart from your mouth, but you shall meditate in it day and night, that you may observe to do according to all that is written in it. For then you will make, your way prosperous, and then you will have good success."

Notice that the Bible says you should meditate upon it "day and night," and in doing so you shall have good success.

Isaiah 26:3 "He will keep in perfect peace whose mind is stayed on Him."

Matthew 6:25-33

"Therefore I say to you, do not worry about your life, what you will eat or what you will drink; nor about your body, what you will put on. Is not life more than food and the body more than clothing? Look at the birds of the air, for they neither sow nor reap nor gather into barns; yet your heavenly Father feeds them. Are you not of more value than they? Which of you by worrying can add one cubit to his stature? So why do you worry about clothing? Consider the lilies of the field, how they grow: they neither toil nor spin; and yet I say to you that even Solomon in all his glory was not arrayed like one of these. Now if God so clothes the grass of the field, which today is, and tomorrow is thrown into the oven, will He not much more clothe you, O you of little faith? Therefore do not worry, saying, 'What shall we eat?' or 'What shall we drink?' or 'What shall we wear?' For after all these things the Gentiles seek. For your heavenly Father knows that you need all these things. But seek first the kingdom of God and His righteousness, and all these things shall be added to you."

Ephesians 3:1-8

If then you were raised with Christ, seek those things which are above, where Christ is, sitting at the right hand of God. Set your mind on things above, not on things on the earth. For you died, and your life is hidden with Christ in God. When Christ, who is our life, appears, then you also will appear with Him in glory. Therefore, put to death your members which are on the earth: fornication, uncleanness, passion, evil desire, and covetousness, which is idolatry. Because of these things the wrath of God is coming upon the sons of disobedience, in which you yourselves once walked when you lived in them. But now you yourselves are to put off all these: anger, wrath, malice, blasphemy, filthy language out of your mouth.

I could go on and on sharing scriptures with you that give credence to the fact that God requires you to give your all. In other words, God requires you to be totally sold out to the kingdom and its principles. God Himself set the example. "For God so loved the world that He gave His only begotten Son;" that's why God asked Abraham for his "only son;" that's why Christ gave His all as "a living sacrifice." Friends, can you see why it is a fallacy to suggest that you could become too heavenly-minded? In fact, I believe we should all observe to do as the Scripture says. There is indeed a high price to pay.

12.1 The Cost

As I mentioned earlier every Christian is called to be a disciple of Christ. The problem is, to be a disciple of Christ will cost you everything. It could cost you your family, your loved ones, your friends—basically, it could literally cost you everything. That is what Paul referred to when he said, "I count all things but loss so that I might win Christ." The question is, are you willing and ready to pay the price? Are you ready to give up everything for the excellence of the knowledge of Christ?

In **Matthew 16:24**: Jesus said, "If any man will come after Me, let him deny himself, take up his cross and follow Me." It means, therefore, that if you want to be a disciple, you must deny yourself, and to deny oneself means to give priority to something or someone over and above your personal needs. For example, you cannot be giving priority to materialism and be sold out to God at the same time. You must remember that it is not about you, it's about Him. This means that Jesus must be given the absolute priority in your life.

How then will this be orchestrated? By taking up your cross and following Him.

In Luke 9:57-62 we read,

> "Now it happened as they journeyed on the road that someone said to him "Lord I will follow you wherever you go." And Jesus said to him, "Foxes have holes and birds of the air have nests, but the Son of Man has nowhere to lay His head." Then He said to another, "Follow Me. "But he said, "Lord let me first go and bury my father." Jesus said to him, "Let the dead bury their dead, but you go and preach the kingdom of God." And another also said, "Lord I will follow you, but let me first go and bid them farewell who are at my house." But Jesus said to

him, "No one having put his hand to the plow, and looking back is fit for the kingdom of God."

As you can see from this passage of scripture, it will cost you your very life to be a true disciple of Christ.

Here are some of the things you can expect to suffer, if you are going to become a true disciple of Christ!

Reproach

If you are going to become a witness for Christ, you will have to be prepared to suffer reproach. Peter said that it was for this very reason we were called. **1 Peter 2:21- 24, 4:13 tells us:**

> "For to this you were called, because Christ also suffered for us, leaving us an example, that you should follow His steps: Who committed no sins, nor was deceit found in His mouth. who, when He was reviled, did not revile in return; when He suffered, He did not threaten, but committed Himself to Him who judges righteously; who Himself bore our sins in His own body on the tree, that we, having died to sin, might live for righteousness—by whose stripes you were healed."

Therefore, just as Christ suffered on a cross of shame, we must suffer likewise. To adopt a cliché, "You have to give up to go up." If you are going to master the art of personal evangelism, you have to give up some things that are dear to you. But listen to **1 Peter 4:13-16:**

> "But rejoice to the extent that you partake of Christ's sufferings, that when His glory is revealed, you may also be glad with exceeding joy. If you are reproached for the name of Christ, blessed are you, for the Spirit of glory and of God rests upon you. On

their part He is blasphemed, but on your part He is glorified. But let none of you suffer as a murderer, a thief, an evildoer, or as a busybody in other people's matters. Yet if anyone suffers as a Christian, let him not be ashamed, but let him glorify God in this matter."

Ridicule

Not only will you have to suffer reproach, but you may also suffer ridicule. This concept is expertly illustrated in **Hebrew 12:2:** "Looking unto Jesus, the author and finisher of our faith, who for the joy that was set before Him endured the cross, despising the shame, and has sat down at the right hand of the throne of God." Notice that it was for "the joy that was set before Him" that He endured the cross. We too must be ready to endure the cross for the joy that awaits us.

Rejection

Earlier I told you that the fear of rejection is one of the greatest stumbling blocks when it comes to witnessing? **1 Peter 2:4 tells us**: "Coming to Him as a living stone, rejected indeed by men, but chosen by God and precious." Well, there is no area of your Christian journey where you are more likely to suffer rejection than you will as a witness. However, you can take comfort in knowing that you have been chosen by God and are precious to Him. Even one hundred percent rejections will be worth it when your heart can finally rejoice and the angels can sing seeing one soul come to salvation.

Death

Yes, you may even have to face death for acknowledging Jesus as your Savior. **Acts 10:34-43 says this:**

Then Peter opened his mouth and said:

> "In truth I perceive that God shows no partiality. But in every nation whoever fears Him and works righteousness is accepted by Him. The word which God sent to the children of Israel, preaching peace through Jesus Christ—He is Lord of all—that word you know, which was proclaimed throughout all Judea, and began from Galilee after the baptism which John preached: how God anointed Jesus of Nazareth with the Holy Spirit and with power, who went about doing good and healing all who were oppressed by the devil, for God was with Him. And we are witnesses of all things which He did both in the land of the Jews and in Jerusalem, whom they killed by hanging on a tree. Him God raised up on the third day, and showed Him openly, not to all the people, but to witnesses chosen before by God, even to us who ate and drank with Him after He arose from the dead. And He commanded us to preach to the people, and to testify that it is He who was ordained by God to be Judge of the living and the dead.'

If you are going to come to that place where you are prepared to suffer reproach, ridicule, rejection, and death, you have to make some significant changes in your life, For instance:-

You Have to Be a New Person

The first change you have to make in your life is to exchange your old life for the new because the old life cannot inherit the kingdom of God. If you are operating in the flesh, which is the old person, there is no way you are going to appreciate these kind of challenges; therefore, you will need to adopt the mind of Christ. **2 Corinthians 5:17** says, "Therefore if anyone is in Christ, He is a new creation; old things have passed away; behold, all things are become new." "All things" mentioned here include a change of mind-set. You have to know you are not the person you once were. The old person you used to be is now dead, replaced by a brand new creation. It is only that new person who will be able to endure such hardship.

You Must Put to Death the Deeds of the Flesh

Putting to death the deeds of the old man can only be done once we become brand new and live in the spirit, putting to death our old desires. **1 Peter 4:1–6 says**:

> "Therefore, since Christ suffered for us in the flesh, arm yourselves also with the same mind, for he who has suffered in the flesh has ceased from sin, that he no longer should live the rest of his time in the flesh for the lusts of men, but for the will of God. For we have spent enough of our past lifetime in doing the will of the Gentiles—when we walked in lewdness, lusts, drunkenness, revelries, drinking parties, and abominable idolatries. In regard to these, they think it strange that you do not run with them in the same flood of dissipation, speaking evil of you. They will give an account to Him who is ready to judge the living and the dead. For this reason the gospel was preached also to those who are dead, that they might be judged according to men in the flesh, but live according to God in the spirit."

12.4 You Must Abide in Christ

John 15:1–17 tells us:

"I am the true vine, and my Father is the vinedresser. Every branch in Me that does not bear fruit He takes away, and every branch that does bear fruit He prunes, that it may bear more fruit. Already you are clean because of the word that I have spoken to you. Abide in Me, and I in you. As the branch cannot bear fruit by itself, unless it abides in the vine, neither can you, unless you abide in Me. I am the vine; you are the branches. Whoever abides in Me and I in him, he it is that bears much fruit, for apart from Me you can do nothing. If anyone does not abide in Me he is thrown away like a branch and withers; and the branches are gathered, thrown into the fire, and burned. If you abide in Me, and My words abide in you, ask whatever you wish, and it will be done for you. By this My Father is glorified, that you bear much fruit and so prove to be My disciples. As the Father has loved Me, so have I loved you. Abide in My love. If you keep My commandments, you will abide in My love, just as I have kept My Father's commandments and abide in His love. These things I have spoken to you, that My joy may be in you, and that your joy may be full. This is My commandment, that you love one another as I have loved you. Greater love has no one than this, that someone lay down his life for his friends. You are My friends if you do what I command you. No longer do I call you servants, for the servant does not know what His master is doing; but I have called you friends, for all that I have heard from My Father I have made known to you. You did not choose Me, but I chose you and appointed you that you should go and bear fruit and that your fruit should abide, so that whatever you ask the Father in My name, He may give it to you. These things I command you, so that you will love one another."

Are You Prepared to Pay the Price?

The big question you have to ask yourself then is this: Am I prepared, willing, and ready to pay the price of discipleship? One of the reasons more of us are not actively involved in the mission field is simply because we are not prepared to pay the price. What are you willing to give up, to go up? Are you willing to sacrifice that relationship? Are you willing to get rid of those material things you hold dear that are preventing you from being effective in your walk with God? Are you willing to be transformed into the image of Christ? You must be prepared to pay the price.

Questions:

1. What is it that you have to be in order to become a witness/ambassador for Christ?

2. Complete the following sentence: The only way you can become an ambassador for Christ is…

3. Name four scriptures that prove you cannot be too heavenly minded!

4. What did the Bible say that God gave to prove that we too need to give our all?

5. What could becoming a disciple of Christ cost you apart from your life?

6. Complete the following Bible verse: If anyone will come after Me...

7. What can a witness for Christ expect to suffer?

8. What significant changes will you be required to make, if you are going to be willing to suffer?

Personal Notes

= CHAPTER THIRTEEN =

Conclusion
Do's and Don'ts
Conditions for Success

Summary of Main Points

For ease of reference, I cannot think of a better way to send you on your soul winning journey than to remind you of a few crucial points we've covered in the previous twelve chapters, along with some do's and don'ts.

First I would like to remind you that, "God has called you out of darkness into His marvellous light; you are a witness of that light." It is therefore up to you to, "Let your light so shine before men that they may see your good works and glorify your Father which is in heaven." Bearing witness of that light is not as difficult as it may appear to be.

You already possess the necessary basic skills and the knowledge required to accomplish the task. But now you must "study to show yourself approved unto God, a workman that needs not be ashamed rightly dividing the word of truth."

As a representative of the kingdom of God you must behave with diplomacy and distinction.

Probably most importantly, if you are going to master the art of personal evangelism, you must have a desire to do it.

It is the duty of every believer, and not just the titled and the gifted to participate in the winning of souls for the kingdom. **(See John 15:16; Matthew 28:19–20.)**

It is God's desire and plan that everyone should be saved. **(See 2 Peter 3:9.)**

Remember that people can only be reached through other people with the exception of the times the Holy Spirit does it Himself.

Conditions for Success

1. You must have a personal experience of salvation (John 15:4–5).
2. You must be an honorable vessel, fit for the Master's use (2 Timothy 2:19–21)
3. You must have a keen interest and love for the word (2 Timothy 2:15).
4. You must lead a life of prayer and worship
5. You must possess a burden and a passion for souls

13.1 Things not to do.

Never assume the "I know it all" attitude

- Never be afraid of anyone, "For God has not given you a spirit of fear but of power and of love and of a sound mind."
- Never lose your cool or become impatient. You must keep a cool head even in the face of severe opposition.
- Never enter into religious mudslinging with anyone; this is not the Clash of the Titans, and you have nothing to prove.
- Never become too personal, especially, when dealing with the opposite sex.

- Don't place any confidence in your own personal ability.
- Don't interrupt others as this may come across as being rude.
- Never enter into doctrinal debates.
- Try not to come on as too overbearing.
- Don't get too hung up on results. Leave the increase to God.
- Be sure not to predetermine or judge anyone because of their lifestyle. Remember, God desires the salvation of all people, and that includes the vilest of sinners.

13.2 Things you must do.

1. You must give yourself time to develop your skills
2. You must purpose in your heart to reach the lost
3. You must show yourself friendly at all times
4. You must be authentic, and;
5. You must be a faithful servant of the Lord

Perseverance is Key.

Perseverance will unquestionably be one of the most important keys to your success as a witness. As I said earlier, you should not place too much emphasis on the immediate outcome of your witnessing; your objective is to sow seeds, not to determine how they grow. If you do not get a positive response, don't worry about it. Here is how Paul explained it to the Church in Galatia: "And let us not grow weary while doing good, for in due season we will reap if we do not lose heart" (**Galatians 6:9**).

May you experience the awesome presence of the Shekinah each and every time you stand to represent the kingdom as an ambassador for Christ.

Personal Notes

_____

_____

_____

_____

_____

_____

_____

_____

_____

_____

_____

_____

_____

_____

_____

_____

_____

_____

_____

_____

ANSWERS TO QUESTIONS

Chapter 1

1. False
2. To be witnesses unto Him.
3. 80%
4. 95%
5. Reasons for the lack of enthusiasm are as follows:
    a. Lack of awareness
    b. Feeling of unworthiness and/or guilt
    c. Ashamed to be identified with Christ
    d. Unaware of the urgency to reach the world for Christ
    e. Lack of preparation
    f. Lack of conviction
    g. Don't know how to witness
6. False.
7. Romans 10:14-17
8. Because of their past.
9. Accusation.
10. Your testimony.
11. The time for harvest is now.
12. 1%
13. Because of society's achievements.
14. True

Chapter 2

1. General and specific.
2. Lack of knowledge, and not knowing our purpose as witnesses.
3. An individual call.
4. A call that is for everyone.
5. Do not believe they are called; Do not have a burden for souls, and; Lack of know how.
6. Listen to hear what God is saying.
7. To be a good listener.
8. He hears the voice of God.
9. Write the vision and make it plain.
10. A call to holiness.
11. Not to strive about words without knowledge.
12. With simplicity.
13. That their faith should not be in the wisdom of men, but in the knowledge of God.
14. He will reject us from being priests for Him.

Chapter 3

1. An ambassador.
2. A representative of a particular country to other nations
3. False
4. With diplomacy and distinction.
5. Diplomacy, maintain good relationship between countries.
6. To maintain good relations between the heavenly and the earthly kingdoms.

7. When in trouble in a foreign country.

8. To help someone get into the kingdom of God.

9. As Christ's ambassadors.

10. Excellent communicators, great problem-solving skills, pleasant personality, builders of relationships between their own country and other nations, focus on the one with whom they are communicating, get their message across as clearly as possible.

11. Diplomacy, professional attitude, not short-tempered, not argumentative and take time and get information right before responding to disagreement.

Chapter 4

1. To rescue the soul from destruction, to tell of the good news of salvation, to testify of what they know about Jesus and to carry out the command of Christ.

2. The wisdom of God in a mystery.

3. <u>Ways Paul acted when he preached to the Corinthians:</u>

   a. He resolved to know nothing among them but Jesus Christ and Him crucified--not theology, not philosophy, not science, and not worldly wisdom.

   b. He purposed in his heart to make a show of no other knowledge than that of Christ.

   c. He determined to preach nothing but Christ and Him crucified.

   d. He was determined to pursue nothing but Jesus Christ. I have read a commentary on this which stated that "Christ in His person and offices, is the sum and substance of the gospel." This then ought to be the subject of any preaching or witnessing. This is powerful stuff.

4. Reasons why we witness:
   a. Because the message of salvation is good news
   b. To testify of what we know about Jesus
   c. Because Jesus commanded us to do so
5. False.
6. False.
7. False.
8. True.
9. False.
10. True.
11. That their faith should not stand in the wisdom of men, but in the power of God.
12. False

Answers to Chapter 5

1. By possessing knowledge or skill in a particular subject.
2. No.
3. The spirit of a servant.
4. A judgmental spirit.
5. To help the lost experience the love of Christ.
6. To go into the entire world, and preach the gospel.
7. He will be with us always even unto the end of the world.
8. To receive power.

Chapters 6

1. Ways to prepare yourself for witness are:
   a. Have to want to do it.
   b. Must be a student of the word.
   c. Must be available.
   d. Must set a good example.
   e. Should never be ashamed of the gospel.
   f. Must stay in control.
   g. Must take it outside your own community.
   h. Must be determined and persistent and;
   i. Will need spiritual wisdom.
2. Doctrinal debates.
3. To bring faith, conviction and salvation into the lives of unbelievers.
4. Excuses.
5. Choose softer targets.
6. Your example.
7. 1% aspiration, 99% perspiration.
8. Opportunity.
9. Spiritual wisdom.

Chapter 7

1. Fear.
2. Fear of rejection and Peer pressure.
3. False Evidence Appearing Real.
4. Let nobody's opinion of you become your reality.
5. Ways fear is likely to affect you:
   a. Will prevent you from being effective.

     b. Will affect your behavior.

     c. Will affect your confidence.

     d. Will prevent you from functioning with courage.

     e. Will prevent you from speaking out.

     f. Will cause you to lack the ability and the capacity to function different from others.

6. Those who care and those who will exploit you.

7. A spirit of fear.

8. Take your rejection as a challenge.

Chapter 8

1. Three basic rules for how to initiate contact:

     a. Change your language.

     b. Choose your targets.

     c. Find a need and fill it.

2. The Good Samaritan.

3. The one that showed mercy to him.

4. Guide answer, that you are being a neighbor to those whom you have mercy.

5. Go and do likewise.

6. To preach the kingdom of God.

7. Power and authority.

8. False.

9. False.

10. That you are interested in the person and to establish a common ground.

11. Water.

12. By simply asking for a drink.

Chapter 9

1. Greek philosophy and Jewish legalism.
2. The love for knowledge.
3. The Holy Spirit.
4. He will tell you what to say in that hour.
5. The Bible.
6. Not to be ashamed of the gospel because it was the power of God or rightly dividing the word of truth.
7. That proper Bible study leads to approval from God.
8. Doctrine, reproof, correction, instruction in righteousness.
9. Honesty.
10. The burden of proof is on them, not you.
11. Help to divert attention.

Chapter 10

1. Reasons why it is difficult to witness to religious Christians are that:
    i.   They know the Bible.
    ii. They know about God.
    iii. They think they are good people, and;
    iv. Doctrinal influence.
2. Sectarianism.
3. False.
4. Luke 9:49-50.
5. You will get into conflicts.
6. The conscience.
7. Praise reports/testimony.

8. <u>The other two ways to witness to people you know are:</u>
   - i. Give them a point of reference.
   - ii. Use the first person approach.
9. Care, understanding and skill.
10. False.
11. The burden of proof is with anyone who says there is no God.
12. Mohammed.
13. The Quran.
14. The Torah, the Zabur and the Injeel.
15. <u>Things Muslims think about Jesus:</u>
   - a. That He was born of a virgin
   - b. Was a great prophet,
   - c. Not a God but only a man,
   - d. Jesus spoke as a baby,
   - e. Heal the sick,
   - f. Raise the dead
   - g. The breath of God
   - h. The spirit of God
   - i. The life of God, The Word of God
   - j. Do not think Jesus died on the cross
   - k. God took Him before He was crucified
   - l. He will return to usher in the final judgment.
16. By performing the five pillars of faith.
17. No. (They believe that their works will be accounted on the Day of Judgment.

Chapter 11

1. <u>The four fundamental principles taught in the Book of Romans are:</u>
   a. Why everyone needs salvation.
   b. How God made the provision for salvation!
   c. How we can receive that salvation, and;
   d. The benefits of obtaining salvation
2. Because some people believe they are good people and do not need salvation.
3. False
4. Because all have sinned.
5. Death
6. False
7. True
8. Believe and confess.
9. Whosoever shall call on the name of the Lord.
10. Being justified by faith we have peace with God.
11. To those who are in Christ.

Chapter 12

1. A disciple of Christ.
2. If you are dead to the flesh and alive in Christ.
3. **Deuteronomy 6:5-6, Joshua 1:7, Matthew 6:25-33 and Ephesians 3:1-8.**
4. His only begotten Son.
5. Your family, your love ones and your friends.
6. Let him deny himself, take up his cross and follow Me.

7. Shame, ridicule, rejection and death.

8. <u>The significant changes you will be required to make, if you are going to be willing to suffer for Christ are:</u>

   - Have to be a new person.
   - Have to put to death the deeds of the flesh.
   - Have to abide in Christ.

NOTES FOR LEADERS

Training people, for the advancement of the gospel as it is with say leading a Bible study, can be a most enjoyable and rewarding adventure life has to offer. However, it can also be very scary—especially if you are embarking on this journey for the very first time. If this describes you, I have some good news for you because you are in good company. When God call Jeremiah to go and preach the gospel, he replied, "Ah, Lord God! I cannot speak"

"Then the word of the Lord came to me, saying: "Before I formed you in the womb I knew you; before you were born I sanctified you; I ordained you a prophet to the nations." Then said I: "Ah, Lord God! Behold, I cannot speak, for I *am* a youth." But the Lord said to me: "Do not say, 'I *am* a youth,' for you shall go to all to whom I send you, And whatever I command you, you shall speak. Do not be afraid of their faces, for I *am* with you to deliver you," says the Lord. Then the Lord put forth His hand and touched my mouth, and the Lord said to me: "Behold, I have put My words in your mouth. See, I have this day set you over the nations and over the kingdoms, to root out and to pull down, to destroy and to throw down, to build and to plant."
Jerimiah 1:4-10

The same was true when God asked Moses to lead the Children of Israel out of bondage in Egypt, he replied, "O my Lord, please send by the hand of whomever *else* You may send." (**Exodus 4:13**). The same was also true for people such as Gideon, Solomon and Timothy and the list goes on. But please note that despite their weaknesses, God helped them tremendously and He will help you as well.

You don't need to be a bible scholar, a teacher or even well versed on the subject of evangelism. The strategy behind these studies is that the leader guides group members to discover for themselves, the principles set out in this study guide together with what the bible has to say about the subject. This method of learning will allow group members to remember much more of what is said than a lecture would.

This study is designed to be led easily. In fact, the flow of questions through the study guide from observation to interpretation to application is so practical that you may feel that the study leads itself. This study guide is also flexible, you can also use it with a number of different groups—bible college students, professionals, church groups etc.

There are some important facts to know about group dynamics and encouraging discussion. The suggestions listed below should enable you to effectively and enjoyably fulfill your role as the group leader.

Preparing for the Study

1. Ask the Lord to help you quickly grasp the concept taught in the particular section and apply it to your own life. Unless this happens, you will not be prepared to lead others. Pray also for the other members of the group. Ask the Holy Spirit to open their hearts to the concept and

accompanying bible texts that will motivate them to action.

2. Read the introduction to the entire guide to get an overview of the entire chapter and the points to be explored.

3. As you begin each study, read and reread the section of the manual "Mastering the Art of Personal Evangelism" together with any relevant bible text so as to familiarize yourself with it.

4. Carefully work through each question in the study. Spend time in meditation and reflection as you consider how to respond.

5. Write your thoughts and responses in the space provided in the study guide. This will help you express your understanding of the section/chapter clearly.

6. Consider how you can apply the relevant scripture to your life. Remember that the group will follow your lead in responding to the studies. They are not likely to go any deeper that you do.

7. Once you have finished with your own study of the section and bible passages, familiarize yourself with the in review of the chapter for the study you are leading together with questions and answer to the questions. These are designed to help you in several ways. First, the questions focus your mind on the concept the author had in mind when preparing the study. Take time to think through how the study questions work to accomplish the purpose. Second, the discussion points and or the in review provide you with a summary of the background to

the chapter to help you focus on the essential aspects. This information can be helpful when people have difficulty understanding or answering questions. Third, the in review can alert you to potential problems you may encounter during the study.

Leading the Study

1. Begin the study on time. Always open with prayer, asking God to help the group to understand and apply the principles and bible texts.
2. Be sure everyone in the group has a study guide if at all possible. Encourage the group to prepare beforehand for each discussion <u>by reading the introduction to the guide and by working through the questions in the study.</u>
3. At the beginning of your first time together, explain that this study is meant to be discussions, not lectures. Encourage the members of the group to participate. However, do not put pressure on those who may be hesitant to speak especially during the first few sessions.
4. You may want to suggest the following guidelines to your group.
    o Stick to the topic being discussed.
    o Your responses should be based on the principle and the scripture reference which are the focus of the discussion and not on external authorities such as commentaries or speakers.
    o Listen attentively to each other and provide time for each person present to talk.

    o   Pray for each other.

5. Have a group member read the introduction at the beginning of the discussion.

6. It is advisable to begin each session with a group discussion question. Chose a question of your choice but one which introduces the theme to the chapter and encourages group members to begin to open up. Encourage as many members as possible to participate, and be ready to get the discussion going with your response.

    This section is designed to reveal where our thoughts and feelings need to be transformed by scripture and concept taught in that section.

    You may want to supplement the chosen question with an icebreaker to help people to get comfortable. Only be sure this ice breaker is pertinent to the section chapter on which you are holding your discussion.

7. Have different group members read aloud the Bible passages referred to at the relevant point during the discussion. Then give people some time to read the passage silently again so they can take it all in.

8. As you ask the questions, keep in mind that they are designed to be used just as they are written. You may simply read them aloud, or feel free to express them in your own words.

    There may be times when it may be appropriate to deviate from the study guide. For example, a question may have already been answered, and, if this is the case, move on to the next question. Also, someone may raise an important question not covered in the study guide. Take time to discuss it, but make sure the group does not go off on a tangent.

9. Avoid answering your own questions, If necessary, repeat or rephrase until they are clearly understood. Or point out something you read in the manual to clarify the meaning of the question. An eager group will easily become passive or silent if they think the leader will do most of the talking.

10. Don't be afraid of silence. People may need time to think about the question before formulating their answers.

11. Do not be content with just one answer, ask, "What do the rest of you think?" or, "is there anything else?" until several people have given answers to the question. Acknowledge all contributions. Try to be affirming whenever possible. Never reject an answer, if it is clearly off target, ask "what has led to that conclusion?" and or what the others think.

12. Do not expect every question to be addressed to you directly. Even thou this will probably happen initially. As group members become more comfortable, they will truly begin to interact with each other. This is one sign of a healthy discussion.

13. Do not be intimidated by controversy, it can be very stimulating. If you do not resolve an issue completely, do not be frustrated, move on and keep in mind for later. The answer may be revealed to you at a later stage.

14. At the end, summarize the study together with what the group has said about the principles shared together with

the relevant Bible passages. This helps to draw together the various thoughts and ideas mentioned and keep the main points fresh in the mind of group members. You may also want to reserve time for the group to practice their evangelistic skills on each other at the end. Or you may want to encourage group members to work on these ideas during the session, and even in their private time.

15. Conclude your time together with conversational prayer. Ask for the help of the Holy Spirit in following through on the commitment you have made to spread the glorious gospel of Christ.

16. It is imperative that you end your session on time.

Now go ahead and apply your new found knowledge and skill in changing the eternal destiny of others or others help others to change the eternal destiny of those in their worlds

AUTOBIOGRAPHY

Glen Kerr is an ordained pastor and founder of Pneuma Life Transformation Ministry Intl. A long time qualified financial professional, he is a graduate of the London Guildhall University and the Brixton Bible Institute London UK respectively. Post graduate in accountancy (Chartered Association of Certified Accountants) ACCA. Association of Accounting Technicians (MAAT), and a honorary MBA, BA (Honors) Degree, and Diploma Higher Education. Glen Kerr has been a Christian for over 35 years and has served in numerous church positions. He has a clear apostolic anointing on his life, confirmed both by word of knowledge/prophecy and a powerful demonstration to that effect. His ministry has taken him to several countries and continents around the world including Europe, The Caribbean, Africa, North America and Asia in an ongoing effort to empower the Body of Christ and to win souls for the kingdom of God. He resides in the UK.

MASTERING *the art of*

Personal

EVANGELISM

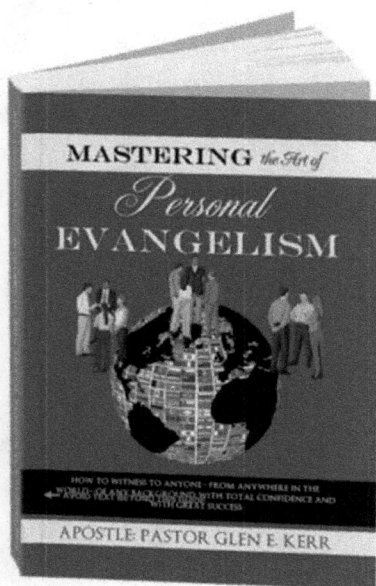

The Spiritual Dynamics

of

EFFECTIVE

LEADERSHIP

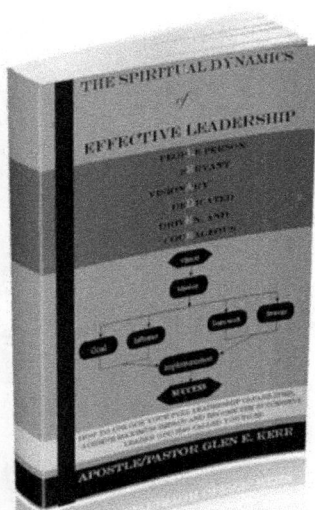

Word of Knowledge Publishing

For further information about this title
Visit www.glenkerr.com
Follow me on Twitter, Facebook and LinkedIn

Personal Notes

Personal Notes

Personal Notes

Personal Notes

Personal Notes

9 789719 596905